Diary of a Traveling Black Woman
A Guide to International Travel

Third Edition

A GUIDE TO INTERNATIONAL TRAVEL

DIARY OF A TRAVELING BLACK WOMAN

D1316172

Nadine C. Duncan

Diary of a Traveling Black Woman

A Guide to International Travel

Nadine C. Duncan

Grace Royal International, LLC

Atlanta, GA

Copyright © 2018 by Nadine Duncan

Published in the United States by: Grace Royal International, LLC.
Atlanta, GA 30316

All rights reserved. No part of this book may be reproduced by an
mechanical, photographic, or electronic process; nor may any parts of
this book be stored in any retrieval system, without the written per-
mission of the publisher—this excludes brief quotations used in reviews.

The intent of the author is to offer general international travel information and motivation to travel. The author assumes no responsibil-
ity for the actions of the reader.

Cover design: Nadine Duncan
Interior Design: Nadine Duncan

ISBN: 978-179132958 (Nadine Duncan)
ISBN: 9781791329358

3rd edition, December 2018
Printed in the United States of America

"The World is a book. Those who do not travel read only a page."

-St. Augustine

For my adventurous mother
Bernadine Atwell

Contents:

The Traveling Bug   11
Traveling Basics   17
The Experience   39
Your Travel Story   71
Start your Journey   81
Travel Resources   107

"And I think to myself, What a wonderful world..."

The Traveling Bug...

It all starts when that friend on social media posts a picture having a blast in a country you never even knew existed. A twinge of jealousy surfaces and immediately you begin thinking of the places you would love to visit but haven't.

The excuses then begin clouding your mind cutting your day dreams short. "If only I had enough money, enough friends, enough vacation days, and enough meds for the plane ride, I would go." It stays on your mind and before you know it, it becomes a dream deferred.

That uncertainty is normal!! Chances are, you've picked up this book expecting to hear only the experiences of someone else. While my experiences are intertwined and I've showcased the experiences of a few other Traveling Black Women, this guide is purposed to help you navigate through the uncertainty of traveling to unknown places and confidently take on the world. As Black women, we should all have the opportunity to travel beyond the US shore and embrace the essence of other cultures. It reminds us of who we are as dynamic individuals and allows us to step outside of ourselves to appreciate all that life has to offer.

TRAVEL BUCKET LIST

☐ _____

☐ _____

☐ _____

☐ _____

☐ _____

☐ _____

☐ _____

☐ _____

☐ _____

☐ _____

☐ _____

☐ _____

☐ _____

☐ _____

☐ _____

☐ _____

☐ _____

☐ _____

☐ _____

☐ _____

☐ _____

☐ _____

☐ _____

☐ _____

☐ _____

☐ _____

Traveling Basics

"It always seems impossible until its done."

-Nelson Mandela

YOU **CAN** TRAVEL

And you **can** afford it!

Here's probably the most important piece of advice you need to start traveling internationally... You **do not** have to break the bank to see the world. Many of us tend to think that traveling is only reserved for those with hefty bank accounts. However, if you really want to experience life beyond these borders, you can definitely make it happen. Of course careful planning and saving is advised, but you can easily look for deals, Groupons, or even volunteer opportunities to whisk you away.

Whether it is a solo trip or group, planning an amazing trip can actually be cheap and easy. Every thing you need to know to plan is at your fingertips online. The Traveling Black Women Facebook group, for example, is full of Black women who bravely ask questions about destinations that they are interested in. Within minutes, other women with experience and recommendations for their interested destination clamor to answer their questions. Many of those women, some of them first time travelers, are able to come back, share photos of an amazing time, and quickly start planning the next trip!

Interacting with Locals & Other Tourists

Just remember that a smile goes a long way in any language! While traveling with friends, even those who were also frequent travelers, I found the staring to be the hard part for many of us. People will stare.... **A lot!** Children may even point. The way I see it, Black women are a symbol of just how talented of a craftsman God is. We are a beautiful mystery to the world. Our hair, our skin, our style, our features, our body, and then the variations among us... Afros, Locs, Perms, Yaki No. 7... We are a gorgeous wonder. You'll find that some folks may even ask to take a picture with you! And really, it's OK!! Have fun with it, or if you aren't comfortable, tell them to scram (nicely of course) and keep it moving.

Our automatic reaction can sometimes be pretty intense. In some cases, we want to know what the *bleep* they are looking at! We immediately feel judged or disrespected by the stares. We become self-conscious of the fact that we are among the only Black Americans around and it's somewhat natural to then assume the worst. In these moments I challenge you to reframe your thinking and consider how much of a gorgeous wonder you are.

Now as always, use your best judgment! I wouldn't advise letting some creepy guy in the corner take a photo of you, but a few folks are truly excited to interact with someone so different. After one week of taking photos with random people in China, I recognized that the attention was as innocent as a baby watching keys jiggle.

You, whether you like it or not, represent the mysteriously strong & beautiful Black Woman! They will wonder how to approach you, how to talk to you, and even make assumptions that you are first cousins with President Obama and Oprah Winfrey. How we react means everything. We cannot take their unfamiliarity with our culture personal. They know as much about our culture as we probably know about theirs. Social Media and TV may be the only vision others have of Black American culture. I'm not saying you *have* to go out there being the spokesperson for Black America. But, remember that you have the power to leave an impression that challenges all preconceived stereotypes.

Chinese Tourists in Cape Town

Personal Space

I'm sure you are thinking... "Really a section on personal space???" Personal space is a characteristic of American culture that we take for granted. Generally, we try not to crowd others when it isn't necessary. We expect to be given space when handling our business in ATM lines, shopping lines, etc. Even when looking for a seat in a waiting room or on public transportation, we tend to skip a seat if we can. It's really almost like a sign of respect for other's space.

Well, everyone else doesn't necessarily see it that way. It simply isn't the norm in some places. Most times, others mean no harm when invading your space. Sometimes they are completely unaware! No need to fuss or get worked up. A polite, "excuse me," usually helps others to realize they are simply too close for comfort.

However, I must keep saying, trust your instincts! Stay vigilant. Be aware of pickpockets or anything that doesn't quite seem right. If you find that someone is unneces- sarily close to you in a wide open space, you may want to step away and look at them a bit crazy.

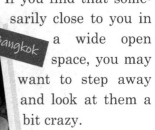

Floating Market in Bangkok

Eating

Carnivore Restaurant—Nairobi

Bring antacids and try everything! Some of us tend to be finicky eaters or at least can name someone who is. We want things a certain way and we love to change the ingredients of an entree on a menu. We also tend to turn our noses up to anything that sounds unfamiliar. For this issue, I have one simple piece of guidance: don't be afraid to try something new.

One of the glorious parts of fully experiencing another culture is their food. Food and how it is consumed is a staple in every culture. It is important that you give the local food at least one try. Generally the locals of any country are excited to share the details of their food with you. It's okay to ask questions and it's okay if you don't like whatever you try, just kindly decline.

If you simply can not handle the local food, you will find that there are almost always familiar fast food places like KFC, McDonald's, and Burger King. You'll also see that the menus are specific to the locale and that in itself could be interesting. If you like, make a note of those differences and share them with your friends when you return home!

The same goes for drinking. Go beyond what you would usually drink back home. Try the local drinks, local beers, or local wines. Attending wine tastings (or bar crawls... depending on your speed) are great ways to meet other travelers and experience the drink of leisure in your host country.

Above all, I'd say use your best judgment. If you haven't eaten red meat in years, for example, now wouldn't be the best time to try bbq ribs no matter how good everyone says they are. Stay hydrated and keep a bottle of water with you. Be sure to bring along indigestion meds, gas tablets, and anything else that you may need to help you deal with the stuff that doesn't agree with you stomach. Most importantly, don't forget to check on the status of the drinking water at your destination!

Bali, Indonesia

Travel Buddies

Ok. This here is a biggie. It can make or break your trip. Pick the crew wisely. Traveling with others presents a situation where you are nearly tied to the hip for a few days. From eating, to sightseeing, to leisure and everything in between, a joint decision is needed to make all parties as comfortable as possible. Don't be afraid to screen the folks that are interested in traveling with you.

This ensures that you are able to make the most of your vacation. This is your time to leave all frustrations behind and lose yourself in another environment. Bring along individuals who compliment your personality and are willing to have a great time!

Once you have selected your traveling crew, plan a tentative itinerary before leaving that everyone can agree on. You don't always have to book tours in advance, but having an idea of what everyone wants to do is best to have beforehand. If you plan to separate or venture off in smaller groups, discuss that beforehand as well. That limits the, "So what you wanna do?"... "Uhhh, I don't care." ...types of conversation. You'll find that without some kind of plan, everyone begins to pass the decision making torch as no one wants to bear the burden of making the wrong decision for the group. Plan ahead as this not only wastes time, but can be quite annoying.

If you are traveling in a large group and plan to separate, I would also advise getting a cheap SIM card for your cell (it must be unlocked). You can usually purchase SIM cards at the airport or at a local mall. This is also helpful for coordinating tours, calling a taxi, etc. and it's much cheaper than using the hotel phone! Communicating via the voice over IP apps when Wi-Fi is available is also a great option.

Dubai, UAE

Or Just Go Alone!

It's also perfectly okay to travel alone. We often think we need to travel with a bunch of friends. However, it is great to travel alone if you have the time, the means, and a great selfie stick. If you've read books like *Eat, Pray, Love*, I'm sure you are aware of exactly how rewarding some alone time abroad can be. Being alone gives you the opportunity to meet new faces and allows you to freely explore without being limited by someone else's preferences.

Of course, safety first! Once you arrive, you don't have to let everyone know you are traveling alone! Stay connected by purchasing a local SIM with data so that you do not have to rely on WiFi for connectivity. Use your discretion in disclosing information about yourself and where you are staying. Be cautious about selecting your accommodations and make sure someone back home is aware of your itinerary.

Currency

After doing research on your specific destination, decide if paper or plastic will be the best mode for you in the country you are visiting. Talk to your bank before leaving. Check to see if there are international transaction fees when you swipe or withdraw money abroad. Let the bank know your travel dates so your card is not stopped for suspicious use. That can be frustrating!! ...Especially, if you can not readily make or receive phone calls!

Always check the exchange rate of the US Dollar to the currency of the country you are traveling to. The rate is based on the economy so there is a chance that the exchange rate can change between the time you book and the time you travel. You can exchange funds online before traveling, at the airport, or any exchange place. Personally, I like to go to the ATM in the airport at the country I've arrived in. For me, it's more convenient to simply pay the ATM fees. Usually I use plastic in hotels, reputable establishments or tour companies, and cash everywhere else (markets, local restaurants, etc.). I'd also advise downloading a currency exchange app to your smart phone for quick reference when needed.

My mother would always say that a dollar is a dollar in a country (and by dollar she meant a single unit of currency). The best example of what is meant by this is seen when you are in a country where USD has more value than the local currency. You may find a local price and a price in USD listed in some touristy spots. The price in USD often looks great at first glance! However when you look at the local price, it is actually far less when you check the exchange rate. You'll also see this when buying bottled water or candy. Needless to say, always carry around local money, and always pay in local money.

When you have the opportunity (in markets for example), bargain! The price you are given is never final until **they** walk away. Lowball!!! You may actually get the price you are looking for!! Again, with local money on hand, this process is usually easier.

It's always good to plan some sort of spending budget. Decide how much you would like to spend on souvenirs, food, and spontaneous sightseeing. When you are checking out Facebook groups and Blogs for your specific travel destination, ask or look for information that will give you a general idea of what prices in that country look like. If you have decided to take a lot of cash for the trip, ration out a daily value for yourself. Keep your daily value with you and lock up the rest in a safe or some hidden area of your hotel room. It's best to travel with an ID (preferably not your passport), the one card you plan to use if necessary, and the cash you aim to spend that day. Make change in your hotel and keep small bills separate so they are easily accessible without revealing your larger bills. In some places, locals can tell an outsider right away by the way they handle their money. This can make you a target. Take a good look at the currency (particularly the coins) before leaving your hotel so you aren't fumbling around in public.

Costa Maya, Mexico

Packing

You do not need half of what you think you do! Pack light!

Packing is probably the most difficult part. Some people wait until the very last minute, while others will have their suitcase sitting by the door a week in advance. Either way you choose, be sure to pack mindfully. Leave a little space for souvenirs, and be sure to check the weight limit for your airline. If you have a lot of friends and family begging you to bring back something other than a magnet or keychain, send them a nice postcard with a personalized "wish you were here" type message. Keep your bags manageable.

Hair items??

Try something with your hair, like a protective style, that would make it easy to manage for a few days (ie. Braids, Faux Locs, a Wet and Wavy Weave, etc.). This limits the fuss over packing flat irons (where electricity can become another issue), liquids, and other hair items.

Shoes??

They add weight to your bag so try to just bring what you *know* you will wear. I know the movies make it seem like everyone is wearing heels in places like London and Paris, but they aren't. Be comfortable—particularly in cities like Barcelona where there is a lot of cobblestone! Select comfortable shoes that will compliment several outfits. If you plan on stepping out into the nightlife, try to coordinate your shoe game with a couple outfits as well. I know it's not ideal if you are a fashionista, but unnecessary baggage can be costly and a huge pain! Not to mention, you may want to save some space to purchase a new exotic pair.

Clothes??

Be sure to check the weather of your destination for the time that you are traveling. Destinations in the Southern Hemisphere (like South Africa & Australia) have completely opposite seasons than we do in America. For warmer climates, I like to do rompers, summer dresses, and leggings. These items are easier to roll and pack than jeans. For cooler climates, I prefer to do sweater leggings or 2-3 pairs of basic jeans and several tops to mix and match with.

Usually we tend to want to go out and shut down the malls before a trip. I still do it as well! Don't go overboard though. Save your coins for the
actual trip! Count your days, look at your itinerary, and

use that to help you plan your day to day wardrobe. You really don't need that many options! Try to find outfits that are easily dressed up or dressed down. For example, leggings, summer dresses, and rompers are my thing because they are cute with accessories and can be pretty versatile.

Packing Hack: Packing cubes are also really helpful gems for rolling your clothes tightly and packing them into neat little cubes in your suitcase. With the right bag and packing cubes, you only need a carry-on sized bag. Be advised that even with a carry-on size, some airlines will weigh your bag and still require you to check the bag.

Electronics??

Place all of your major electronics (camera, laptop, tablets, etc.) in your hand luggage. You may have to remove it at TSA so keep it accessible. Be sure to grab a travel adapter before leaving—plugs and voltage differ per country. Grab one before you go from a local department store because the airport prices are crazy! I have one friend that travels with a universal strip (three or four outlets that fits every plug.) I laughed at her until our trip to Sri Lanka when I realized our room had limited outlets and I had to use one of hers.

Lost Luggage??

Personally, I prefer to use a carry on if I can... and most of the time, I can! I really do not like to check luggage. I traveled for 21 days in Asia (Hong Kong, Philippines, China, and Japan) with a carry on and a backpack. I used the coin laundry and a sample pack of detergent at my hotels to wash my clothes.

If you prefer to check your bag, grab a lock, double check the airport code on the tag during check in. I'd advise a lock, a nametag, and an identifying ribbon or sticker (especially if it is black). I can't say this will guarantee the airline's luggage efficacy, but it will certainly lessen the chances of someone mistakenly walking off with your bag or your bag being sent to the wrong place.

Toiletries??

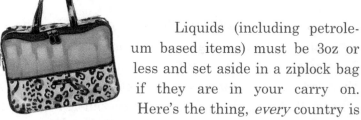

Liquids (including petroleum based items) must be 3oz or less and set aside in a ziplock bag if they are in your carry on. Here's the thing, *every* country is different about how strict they are with this rule. You may get to Heathrow and be sent through the wringer for a sample size tube of mascara like I was, or you may walk through other security lines with a whole 8oz tube of lotion that you forgot was in your purse. Because we never know who is going to be aiming for employee of the month that day or who doesn't care, I advise you to err on the side of caution. You don't want to have to throw away costly items.

Most grocery stores and pharmacies have ready made travel bags and tubes to put your lotions, soaps, etc. in; however, if you plan on checking your bag you don't have to worry about a thing. Keep in mind that larger toiletries can also add unnecessary weight! Decide if you really need that 16oz bottle of lotion or 12oz bottle of sunscreen.

Consider your make up bag as well. Unless you are heading on a work assignment as a make-up artist, you do not need the whole kit and caboodle. I'd advise getting a travel makeup bag to take only the makeup you are most likely to use.

TSA

Even with TSA Precheck, long lines and general foolishness going through security are exactly why arriving two hours before your flight is necessary!! In general, there are certain things you can not take on a flight anywhere. To be on the safe side, check out the full list at **www.tsa.gov**. If you are taking your everyday purse, check it for sharp items or lotions you may have forgotten about before you go!

Every airport and every TSA employee is different. Therefore, if you happen to get to point B with your shears or razors, but then have it taken from you at another check point, the argument that the last check point let you through is a moot point. My mother, for example, left Abu Dhabi a happy camper with all her creams and perfumes in her carry-on. When she arrived to her layover in Heathrow, they stripped her of most of her items (even though they were all under 3oz) and stated that she had "too many." Therefore, I advise you to err on the side of caution for an easier process.

Similarly, be prepared for most places to ask you to remove your electronics, shoes, belt, jewelry, scarf, and jackets. Dress in a manner that allows you to remove items and redress easily. Do not let going through security add additional stress to your journey. Pack wise, dress wise!

Customs

DO NOT take photos at customs. And in some cases, you are not even allowed to be on your phone (some places are more lenient than others). I know it is difficult to resist the temptation to start taking pics as soon as you land, but look out for no photo signs.

Be careful about what you are trying to bring back into the US. Fruits, vegetables, plants and animals are a firm no. When completing your Customs questionnaire, more than likely you will have nothing to declare. Your souvenirs are usually of no concern to the customs agents.

The lines at Customs can be pretty long, especially when returning to the United States. Download the Mobile Passport or apply for Global Entry to ease your re-entry to the States (think of it as TSA Pre-Check for Customs).

Duty-Free Hack: If you make an alcohol purchase at Duty-Free and end up with a connecting flight or long lay over in the US (for example, flying into Miami from Spain and then flying home to Atlanta hours later), you do not have to pack it! Request a sealed Duty Free Bag. TSA will open it on the layover, check the receipt and contents with a swab and send you on your way. The purchase, however, must have been completed less that 48 hours prior.

The Flight

This is the part many of us are worried about. The anxiety is normal. However, statistics show that there is a greater likelihood of you being in a car accident than a plane crash.

If you are especially nervous, there is no shame is closing your eyes and taking a moment to talk to your God in whatever way that works for you; even if its just a moment of expressing gratitude for the means to travel and return.

For shorter flights (4 hours or less), a movie, a good book, a couple of magazines, and even a coloring book can help pass the time. As for me, I'm most likely fast asleep until I hear the snack cart rolling through. For longer flights, I love to watch all kinds of movies... including foreign movies with subtitles. You'd be surprised how good some of them are.

On longer flights, you want make it a habit to move around often. Go see what the folks in the other cabins are doing!

Stay hydrated—especially if you are indulging in the free wine like I do. Compression socks (a MUST beyond 7 hours), will help keep your legs from cramping up and feeling like rubber once you stand up. If you are concerned about plane food, bring your own snacks, and/or find the flight attendant that will give you extra snacks from their attendant stash.

Packing Checklist

☐ Passport

☐ Unlocked Cellphone (Optional for connectivity using a local SIM Card with data as opposed to relying on WiFi, or purchasing an International Plan).

☐ Snacks

☐ 3oz Toiletries

☐ Probiotics / Antacids

☐ Ibuprofen /Aspirin

☐ Chargers

☐ Universal Adapter (If Necessary)

☐ Luggage Tag

☐ Luggage Lock (For Checked Bags)

☐ Packing Cubes

☐ Compression Socks

☐ Draws

☐ Toothbrush

☐ This Book

Better to see something once, than to hear about it a thousand times.

—Asian Proverb

The Experience

What experiences are on your life list?

(ie. SkyDiving in Dubai, Hiking in Peru, Scuba Diving in Australia)

☐ _____

☐ _____

☐ _____

☐ _____

☐ _____

☐ _____

☐ _____

☐ _____

☐ _____

☐ _____

☐ _____

☐ _____

- [ ] _____
- [ ] _____
- [ ] _____
- [ ] _____
- [ ] _____
- [ ] _____
- [ ] _____
- [ ] _____
- [ ] _____
- [ ] _____
- [ ] _____
- [ ] _____
- [ ] _____
- [ ] _____

Every experience is different.
You, and only you, create your story.
Here is a just little info to get you started...

Paradigm Shift

Whether you are deciding to travel for business, pleasure, or both, get ready to spend some time indulging in the ambience of a different environment. Now, there are some of us that always think we know how something should be. Some of us can be a little judgmental when things are unfamiliar. You know we've all started a phrase or two with "They should have just..." or ended a phrase with "...cause that's just too much like right."

When faced with unfamiliar situations we have to remember that we are not only in a different country but we are also among a different culture. This means that perceptions and mindsets will be **very** different from our own. What is a norm for us, may not be a norm for the culture you are visiting. This is a great opportunity to reflect on some of the things we take for granted and learn from another culture.

That being said, I'm not asking you to gloss over an obviously racist or sexist situation, but I am asking you to be open minded when considering cultural norms. The best way to deal with confusing scenarios is simply to take it in, make a mental note, **adjust your perspective**, and keep it moving... Don't be that person who projects that their way is the only way, or the right way. Be the person who stepped out of their comfort zone long enough to recognize there is more to the world.

In this section, I'll give you a brief idea of what you can expect while traveling. It is important to remember that everyone, even people on the same trip, will have different experiences. Be careful of making decisions based *solely* on someone else's opinion or experience. It's best to see everything for yourself.

Visas

Always check the visa information for your country prior to arrival. Many countries do not require you to have a Visa before arriving if you have an American passport. Some countries simply stamp your passport with a visa while others may give you a full page sticker. Be sure to check the prices for visas before hand!! My sorors and I were shocked when we showed up to Tanzania and were asked to pay $100 USD for a mandatory annual visa! Yikes!

Countries such as Russia and China require you to go through a formal Visa application process well before arriving. For this process, I'd recommend going to an International Visa business in your area and letting them handle the process.

Maasai Mara Kenya

Africa

Africa is a beautifully diverse continent. You can indulge in historical sites, beaches, animal safaris, amazing food, and a myriad of varying cultures—some of which have been graciously untouched by the rest of the world and our shenanigans.

Africa is so much more than what is often portrayed in the media than groups of communities needing to be saved. In reality, Africa is the continent that drives the entire world's existence... But, that's another story for another book.

Different vaccinations and medications (i.e. Malaria Pills) are required for travel into many countries within Africa. Prior to traveling, it is important to research the vaccinations required for your specific travel area (http://travel.state.gov). Some vaccinations and medications require you to be vaccinated for a certain amount of time before traveling. Some countries, like Tanzania, will require you to show proof of vaccination upon entry. You can request a vaccination book/card from your doctor or clinic and keep it with your passport.

Europe

As a Black woman, you may receive a lot of stares and occasional flirting from curious older European men. You *may* encounter a few racist individuals here and there. But, **do not** allow that to discourage you from venturing out and seeing what you want to see. With that in mind, be sure to smile, greet, and/or reach out to the other Black travelers that you may see in a sea of European faces. It always bothers me when I see other Black women who are traveling, yet avoid making eye contact to say a quick hello. I'm not sure why that is, but it's important that we make connections... especially in a foreign country.

Europeans generally tend to be laid back. Outdoor cafés are perfect for people watching, sipping wine, and taking a moment to take in the new surroundings. Public transportation (ie. metro, street car, taxi) is widely used. Cars are generally smaller and a large number of people travel by bicycle or scooter. If you like history, or are just interested in the roots of the surrounding culture, check out the local museums!

Middle East

Black women, myself included, have been leaving the US to work and live in this region. Our presence is pretty strong out there now than when I initially moved there in 2010. The one key thing to keep in mind about the Middle East is modest dress. While it may be hot as Hades, appropriate summer wear is slightly different than what we are used to in the United States.

Note that Dubai is a bit more lax than the rest of the region, but there are still clear expectations for modesty in places like the Dubai Mall. Always bring a scarf or cardigan with you just in case.

Bali, Indonesia

Asia

Asian countries are full with so much culture and great food. From the exotic beaches of Southeast Asia to the city lights of Tokyo, Asia is also an immensely diverse continent. As a black woman, you will definitely stand out in most Asian countries. They are going to be clamoring to take photos with you and at times it can be annoying and uncomfortable, but a firm "No!" will send many intrusive travelers on their way.

Australia/New Zealand (Oceania)

This region is in the southern hemisphere so their seasons will be the opposite of the United States. The waters there are spectacular. This is the best place in the world for snorkeling and deep sea diving. Absolutely breathtaking! You must bring a waterproof camera! Make sure you also take a moment to experience the Aboriginal culture and learn about their history.

West Indies

The islands of the West Indies are amazing! The crystal blue Caribbean waters are so warm and inviting. Expect to relax and go with the flow. Cruises are a great way to sample a number of islands in one

Trinidad Carnival

vacation. You will find that a lot of islands will have visual similarities, but you will see the uniqueness in the food and culture of the locals. **If you have never traveled internationally, the Caribbean is the best place to start.**

Although the twin islands of Trinidad and Tobago have the best Carnival in the West Indies *(yes I'm biased),* just about every Caribbean Island has an annual Carnival celebration that is worth taking part in. IMO, this is the best time to get a true taste of the West Indian Culture.

Central/South America

This region is an assortment of beautifully diverse countries with truly gorgeous people. The African Diaspora is so beautifully entrenched with the culture of this region. When traveling to this region, be sure to spend a day exploring Afro Latino/Latina cultures. As with most regions of the world, the history and insight of the indigenous people are astonishing.

Be sure to do your research on your specific country of interest as there are particular areas that require you to stay vigilant and exercise modesty as an American tourist. It's a good idea to book reputable, licensed tours prior to arriving.

Other than that, you'd be surprised at what the African Diaspora looks like here. You will encounter many different Black people who look like someone you know until you realize they don't speak much English. Countries like Belize, Brazil, and Panama do an amazing job of reminding us of how vast, diverse, and magical the African diaspora is.

Havana, Cuba

The ^{New} 7 Wonders of the World

How many have you seen?

☐ Great Wall of China (China)

☐ Christ the Redeemer Statue (Brazil)

☐ Machu Piccu (Peru)

☐ Chichen Itza (Mexico)

☐ The Roman Colosseum (Italy)

☐ Taj Mahal (India)

☐ Petra (Jordan)

Need Specific Advice?

Join the

Traveling Black Women

Facebook Group!

 #TravelingBlackWomen

The experiences of

#travelingblackwomen

I've always been comfortable spending time alone/with myself and with others so day to day varies. I could sightsee or roam alone or connect with someone or people on the way. There are tons of ways to connect with people before you arrive and when you're at your destination and I make sure I have one connection lined up for most trips. For the most part I've felt safe traveling alone. I'm cautious at night of course; I don't get sloppy drunk or share too many details with strange people about my plans. I am a bit adventurous and maybe a little too trusting at times, but I'm a good judge of character and use my intuition when in unfamiliar situations. Plus I'm not going to war zone or unsafe places. I've only stayed in hostels twice. While you can meet people, it's not really my preferred accommodation. I like to rent apartments/vacation rentals/villas or just stay in a hotel depending on my budget and how long I'll be around. There are definitely times I would have loved to have certain friends with me for some of these experiences, but I don't regret traveling alone at all. For me going solo and having those experiences, making new friends/contacts etc. makes it all worthwhile.

Absolute Travel Addict
April Danielle

Our differences are all rooted in our sameness...

Mursi Tribe, Omo Valley, Ethiopia December 2012

I took a solo trip to South Omo Valley in Ethiopia for New Years. This had to have been one of the most beautiful experiences of my life. I visited several different tribes, all distinct in their own way. I traveled to a place of living ancient people holding firm to their traditions while embracing some of the spoils of the modern world. No matter which corner of the world I reach, I always come back to being humbled and in awe of the human race.

Tiaya Daniels—Atlanta,GA

"South Africa was amazing! The people...the landscape...everything was beautiful. The fact that it was so rich in history catered to the history nerd in me. Visiting the Apartheid museum, learning about Nelson Mandela...I loved it. South Africa was definitely one of my favorite trips!"

Raenice Weakly—Houston, TX

I arrived at the hotel, which was gorgeous and down the street from the hottest night strip I've ever seen: Bars, clubs, loud music, Ping Pong Shows, food, shopping, Lady Boys galore and so much more!

Day 1

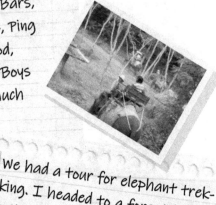

We had a tour for elephant trekking. I headed to a forest-like destination around 8:30am. I enjoyed a monkey, elephant and Thai boxing show. I also went to a Thai cooking demonstration where I cooked my first ever Papaya Salad. It was sooo delicious! BUT! The last thing I did before leaving that tour was to ride around the forest on an elephant--a freaking elephant!!!!! It was amazing! The elephants were huge and very friendly. I was even able to get my very first elephant massage.

Day 2

Day 3

I headed to Phi Phi Island where the movies, James Bond and Beach, were filmed. The view was nothing but spectacular!

Day 4

Shopping!! Bargain, bargain, bargain because their final price isn't their final price!!! My last day in Thailand, I got the famous Thai massage from a small spot on Patong Beach. A Thai massage is a must to get before leaving Thailand! I had the best time I've had in years! You don't need a visa if you're an American, make sure that you arrange airport pickup, and look around to different places before booking any tours because more than likely you can get better deals than your first offer. Have fun!!!

Shelley Wolfe—Allendale, SC

The first time I went abroad was two years after I graduated from college. My biggest regret during my college years was not studying abroad, so I decided to move to France for a year to teach English. I remember packing my suitcases worried that I was moving to a country I had never been and where I wouldn't know a soul. To make matters worse, I had not figured out housing arrangements for when I arrived in France. I thought, "I'll figure it out when I get there." At first it was hard adjusting to a different life and culture than I was accustomed to, but I thrived and survived! After a few months of living and traveling throughout France, I was hooked. I made friends from all the around the world. One of my favorite memories is the time I, and two friends, decided to go on a roadtrip through the wine country of France. Our only shared language was French, which we all spoke at a very rudimentary level (if that)...

Daniele Wilson—Amityville, NY

When I lived in Abu Dhabi, I would always look at my friends and think, "If I was back in the United States, I would not be friends with half of the people here." At first I considered that a bad thing, but as time went on and bonds began to grow, I realized how fortunate I was to be plucked from everything and everyone I know, to have an opportunity to grow and learn more about myself while learning about others.

I am proud to say today that through my travels I have made Jewish, Muslim, Christian, Atheist, Black, White, Brown, and friends everywhere in between.

I have learned to step out of my box and try new things, whether that be frog legs in France, Camel Burgers in Abu Dhabi or Ostrich Steaks in Kenya.

I have learned to go with the flow and never sweat the small stuff.

I have also learned that there are people out there with views and beliefs so much more different than anything I could every have imagined.

I have learned to accept and realize that my way of believing and doing things is just that, MY way.

Most importantly I have learned that everything that matters to me in this life can fit into two 23kg suitcases and two carry on bags.

Andreka Lattimore—Sandersville, GA

I AM HERE
NANZHUGAN HUTONG
BEIJING, CN

"The world is full of beauty and adventure...eat the food, embrace the customs, respect the religions, and love the people...Travel"

Kabrina Johnson—Houston, TX

This was by far the most relaxing vacation I ever had, and could have been a romantic one if I had traveled with a man. Lol! But, I totally understood why Prince William and Kate honeymooned there. The Seychelles offers activities during the day and peace and quiet at night. Get yourself a private driver and explore the main part of the island in a day. You can climb granite hills to get awe inspiring views, visit their National Park to take in gorgeous flora and fauna. If you're brave enough, giant tortoises are everywhere and you can easily hop into pens to feed them.

When you're ready to step away from the main part of the island, a quick boat trip is all it takes. You then can walk into a new world of white sand beaches and turquoise waters, nature hikes, natural spring waters, creole food, coconut shacks, and fruit bats. It's not a popular destination site for people who look like me, but it's a place where the locals look like me. So visiting my creole brothers and sisters was an awesome experience.

Jebel Shams—Oman's Grand Canyon

Challenging expectations

Choosing one destination isn't always the easiest task to do. I've been on many wonderful trips and I do mean many. I've been blessed to see very different places and there are still so many I'd still like to see.

I live in Abu Dhabi and decided to go to Oman on my last journey. At the recommendation of a friend, we traveled beyond the UAE border to Jebel Shams. This was a road trip adventure and a bit of a surprise to me! It was not extremely exotic but I found it to be equally as awesome as any other place I've been to. Jebel Shams is referred to as the Grand Canyon of Oman and it was a thrill to see people actually living within it. There were houses, built up shacks, and caves that I just did not expect.

Tracey Smith - Brooklyn, NY

LaJohna Carter – Carthage, TX

BARCELONA
CITY MAP
FREE

Traveling Solo to Barcelona

I traveled to Barcelona, Spain March 2013. I decided to travel alone because I wanted to visit a place that others weren't able to visit due to other obligations. The experience was a fabulous one. I was never bored. I did the "Hop On Hop Off" tour which could easily be an all day event. I actually did the 2-day tour. The only thing I felt I missed out on was the nightlife due to not wanting to go out alone.

A Beautiful Sistah in South Korea

My first overseas placement was located in Uijongbu, South Korea. This experience had a major impact on my life for many reasons. However, as an educator this experience taught me how to build closer relationships with my students, flexibility, patience, and how to think and teach beyond the normal standards. In the Korean culture education and educators are highly recognized and honored. Parents expect you to show a great amount of love and dedication to each and every one of the students in the form of teaching, hugging, listening, and encouragement. All of the parents were actively involved with their child's education and implemented all suggestions from the teacher to help their children excel in education. The children's view on education mirrored that of their parents. Therefore, they performed above and beyond my initial expectations. This showed me the true ability children have when it comes to discipline and learning.

During my journey I was also faced with many challenges. These challenges included language barriers between my co-workers, students, parents, the general public, and myself. In an effort to build a solid relationship with my students and communicate more effectively with my parents, I decided to learn how to read, write, and speak the basic Korean language. This proved my ability to do whatever it took to be an effective teacher in the classroom. I was extremely proud of myself and so were my students!

Another challenge I was faced with was when the administration at my school announced that all teachers were responsible for writing, directing, and producing an end of the year performance/play to showcase their students' English-speaking growth for the year. This made me very nervous because I was indeed confident in my teaching ability, however, not so much in producing a performing arts drama. I had five months to get the entire production ready. I was working with 11 seven year old students who had only been speaking English for one year. I decided to remake the musical "Annie." I gave each student eight lines to remember in the play for their character. They were also asked to learn four complete songs from the movie. We practiced day after day and to my amazement they performed like little stars on the big stage. At this point I was overjoyed with my student and myself for putting on such a great show!

This wonderful opportunity that I have had has revealed to me my ability to do any and everything I put my mind to. I personally have performed above and beyond my own expectations as an educator. I really love the way the Korean people value education. It reminds me just how important my job as an educator is and why I love it so much. These individuals have opened my eyes and allowed me to see life from a completely different perspective. It was an experience of a lifetime and I am truly grateful to have gotten this opportunity.

Checkout my blog "A Beautiful Sistah in South Korea" to read about my day-to-day experiences.
Be sure to start from the beginning!
http://blairy85.blogspot.com

Don't just visit a place, but try to learn something about their culture, language, and people. Open yourself up to the possibilities that exist outside of your comfort zone...

You'll never know who you may meet, and the ways in which they will impact your life...

Jacelyn Matthews—Hillside, NJ

I love a good jumping photo op!

Nadine plans her next trip.

"Perhaps travel cannot prevent bigotry, but by demonstrating that all peoples cry, laugh, eat, worry, and die, it can introduce the idea that if we try and understand each other, we may even become friends."

– Maya Angelou

Your Travel Story

Now that you've gotten an idea of what international travel is like, let's start planning!
The purpose of this book is to encourage Black women to travel internationally. Therefore, this is not my diary. This is yours. Use these pages to freely record ideas, options, confirmation numbers, etc.

Where are you going? Why?

Knowing "why" you want to travel to a particular place is important when planning your experience.

When?? For how long??

Be sure to research the climate and seasonal rates for the time period you want to go... Consider neighboring countries that you may want to visit while in the vicinity.

Who are you thinking of taking with you? Why?

Travel buddies can make or break your experience.
Choose carefully or go solo!

Notes:

Flight Info/Options

1. Determine the name of the international airport at your location. Check to see if there is more than one airport so you can compare prices. (For example, flights into Orly are often less expensive than flights into Charles De Gaulle when traveling to Paris, France.)

2. Use an online booking engine to help you locate your ticket. **However,** once you have found a ticket that fits your budget and traveling needs (i.e. short layover, non-stop, etc.), check the official website of the airline. In some cases you will find that the price on the airline website is the **SAME or LESS** than the prices on the 'discount' sites. If that is the case, purchase the ticket directly from the airline. This will also eliminate third-party issues in the event of any problems on travel day.

3. Book!

   a. Pay careful attention to dates and times as the change in time zones may cause you to lose a day. (I have known plenty of friends to show up to the airport at midnight on the wrong day. That can be a hassle!!!)

   b. Pay attention to layover (length, location, and quantity). Sometimes, when looking for the cheapest flight, we may overlook the 9 hour layover, or the 30 minute layover (which almost always puts you in a position to miss your flight or rush through the airport looking crazy #stressful).

c. Long layovers (9-24hours) can be exciting if they are in a city that you want to visit briefly or simply have lunch in. Take a cab ride, train ride, or even book a "layover tour." Be mindful of your time though! You don't want to miss your connecting flight.

d. Red-Eye flights (late-night flights) are actually good for jet-lag if you can sleep through the whole flight.

Lodging Info

a) Traditional Hotels (use online booking engine), Rent Apartments (vacation rental sites), Hostels (check reviews online)

b) Research local hotel chains. They may not always show up in an online booking search. Local hotels in Europe, for example, are small but often less expensive, elegant, and comfy.

c) List address, check in time, contact information for location, airport transportation

d) Always take the taxi at the taxi stands... not the shady looking guys inside the airport saying "Taxi? Taxi?" Rideshare (ie. Uber, Lyft) may or may not be available.

e) Research the location of your hotel. Is it central to where you would like to be? Cheaper hotels may be further away from the action but the cost of transportation from the outskirts may end up costing you the same (or more) as booking a centrally located hotel that allows you to walk or take shorter cabs rides.

f) Always check the amenities so there are no surprises when you arrive. (i.e. Free Wifi may only be available in the Lobby and not your hotel room.)

g) Get points from your stay!

h) Always Read, Read, Read the Reviews!!! Look for the most recent reviews as some hotels do make changes after receiving negative feedback. As you read through the reviews you will notice a common thread after the first 3-5 posts. That will let you know whether or not it is a place you would want to stay.

Tours / Sightseeing

What are the main attractions you'd like to see? Research the best tour companies using the blogs and/or travel groups. Booking attractions through travel sites can occasionally be more expensive than finding a reputable local company. Shop around a little bit and get the best bang for your buck.

There are some things that are free to visit but expensive when included in a tour. Decide what will work best for you considering transportation and navigating around town. Just be aware that tourists prices are often inflated so get online and ask!

Booking tours in advance is not always necessary but definitely advised for a smooth vacation. I book in advance depending on my travel group or when I feel like there is a lot I want to see and a short span of time to see it in.

I'd advise you to:

a) Write out a daily plan (it doesn't have to be stringent... just a list of ideas to guide what you want to do and when.)

b) Consider what is a "must see" for you of all the possible attractions.

c) After booking tours or activities, write down the contact name, number, and booking confirmation.

d) As with lodging, **Read, Read, Read Reviews!!!!**

Start your Journey!

_____

_____

_____

_____

_____

_____

_____

_____

_____

_____

_____

_____

_____

_____

_____

_____

_____

_____

_____

_____

_____

_____

_____

_____

_____

_____

_____

_____

_____

_____

_____

_____

_____

_____

_____

_____

_____

_____

_____

_____

_____

_____

_____

_____

_____

_____

_____

_____

_____

_____

_____

_____

_____

_____

_____

_____

_____

_____

_____

_____

_____

_____

_____

_____

_____

_____

_____

_____

_____

_____

_____

_____

_____

_____

_____

"You can hear other people's wisdom , but you've got to re-evaluate the world for yourself."

-Mae Jemison

Resources

Websites, Blogs, Groups, Etc.

The Internet and networks like The Traveling Black Women Facebook Group are great resources for everything you need to know about getting ready to travel!

"Discount" Booking Sites

Flight and Hotels

⇒ www.kayak.com

⇒ www.priceline.com

⇒ www.orbitz.com

⇒ www.expedia.com

⇒ www.cheapoair.com

⇒ www.lastminutetravel.com

⇒ www.howire.com

⇒ www.skyscanner.net

Hotels/Vacation Rentals Only

⇒ www.agoda.com

⇒ www.hotels.com

⇒ www.booking.com

⇒ www.airbnb.com

⇒ www.flipkey.com

⇒ www.homeaway.com

⇒ www.trippin.com

⇒ www.vrbo.com

Travel References

Gov't Travel Websites

⇒ www.tsa.gov

⇒ travel.state.gov

⇒ www.usa.gov

Travel Resources & Guides

⇒ www.travelingblackwomen.com

⇒ www.lonelyplanet.com

⇒ www.fodors.com

⇒ www.tripadvisor.com

⇒ www.frommers.com

⇒ www.worldtravelguide.net

⇒ travel.usnews.com

⇒ www.weworktotravel.com

and more...

There is so much more I'd like to share, but my purpose is not to overwhelm you with information that may not be applicable to your trip. My purpose is to inspire you to get out there and see the world.

I encourage you to use the resources here to learn all you can about the places you'd like to visit and then go. I can't guarantee you that everything will always go smoothly, but I can guarantee you personal growth, awesome pics, and social media check-ins that will make your friends jealous.

P.S. The crazy stuff that happens always makes for a great story later!!

About the Author

Nadine C. Duncan is an educator, student, and travel enthusiast who has been blessed to visit over forty countries and counting. She was born in New Jersey to Trinidadian parents and grew up traveling to the West Indies every summer. Those awesome summers allowed Nadine to develop a deep appreciation for similarities and differences of the Trinidadian and American cultures.

At the age of 27, Nadine moved to Abu Dhabi, UAE and resided there as an educator for a little over three years. That experience fortified her appreciation of different cultures and motivated her to visit countries she never expected to.

Nadine currently resides in Atlanta, GA where she is an educator and Founder of The PrOOF Project, Inc. She plans to continue traveling and exploring while inspiring other women to do the same.

Follow her journey and others on Instagram @travelingblackwomen

Go live your BEST life!

www.travelingblackwomen.com

#travelingblackwomen

Grace Royal Atwell
My Granny, the original traveler.
1936—2017

CPSIA information can be obtained
at www.ICGtesting.com
Printed in the USA
LVHW081647230419
615097LV00022B/307/P

9 781791 329358